21 ways to FORGIVE

Plus Nine Reasons We Must Forgive

FULLY ILLUSTRATED

Books For Prisoners Project

Gospel Net Ministries sends boxes of this book, 21 WAYS TO FORGIVE to chaplains who work in America's prisons and jails. The chaplains give this book to the men and women they minister to. Over 7,000 copies of 21 WAYS TO FORGIVE have been donated and placed in prisons across the U.S.A. Chaplains love it and are asking for many more. It will soon be available in Spanish.

We discount the books to approximately three dollars each for sponsors. A donation of $100 has been sufficient to pay for thirty books plus media rate shipping. This pricing is subject to change but a $100 donation, even with inflation, is a good target number for donors. We usually start with a box of thirty books but we continue to send as many as a chaplain requests and as often as they request as God helps us.

Because America's prison system is the largest in the entire world with over two million inmates we need many more sponsors. Sponsoring a chaplain is a great way to bring glory to God and help to people. You can donate online at www.EncouragementExpert.com or send a check to Gospel Net Ministries, PO Box 485, Creswell, OR 97426. Write "Books for Prisoners" in the memo of your check. You can phone Wes Daughenbaugh directly at 541-729-5015 to sponsor books or order them for a class you might teach in your church or small group.We will give you the Teacher's Guide for free as well as a free DVD of Wes teaching through it if you order fifteen books. Pricing for churches and individuals (not prisons) remains at a discounted price of $5 per book.

WHAT CHAPLAINS ARE SAYING ABOUT 21 WAYS TO FORGIVE

This book is an extraordinarily poignant and life changing resource. It provides a powerful faith based comprehensive approach to becoming and staying free of the bondage of unforgiveness. I highly recommend it to chaplains, pastors, and others in leadership and guidance as a practical very helpful reference to those you serve!
Chaplain Ronald Cooper, Western New Mexico Correctional Facility

21WAYS TO FORGIVE is an excellent book. It cuts straight through to the heart and appeals to the conscience. I took the opportunity to read 21 WAYS TO FORGIVE just before distributing it to some of the inmates here and it was a tremendous blessing to me as well as to them. Wes obviously writes from his own personal experience, which makes the book an easy read. The content is Christ-like, Biblical and opens the door to genuine healing which is certainly needed among the inmate population. I give 21 WAYS TO FORGIVE a FIVE STAR rating and highly recommend it to anyone looking to deepen their relationship with Christ and their fellow man.
Chaplain Marvin Johnson, Central Mississippi Correctional Facility

I think your book, 21 Ways To Forgive, is absolutely awesome; it is so easy to read and is filled with excellent encouraging ways to receive peace of mind and soul. I truly believe that it will be a true inspirational reading for our incarcerated individuals here at the Fort Dodge Correctional Facility. I'm anxious to get these books here. It's just what we need.
Paula Addison, spiritual coordinator, Fort Dodge Correctional Facility, Fort Dodge, Iowa

Recently you sent to my prison copies of the book, "21 Ways To Forgive." **The response to this book has been very positive. In fact, all the copies went out like pancakes.** Might you be able to give us more copies?
Chaplain Gil Alden, Washington State Penitentiary, Walla Walla, WA

21 ways to FORGIVE

Plus Nine Reasons We Must Forgive

FULLY ILLUSTRATED

WES DAUGHENBAUGH

REDEMPTION
PRESS

Illustrated by David Wilson
Cover Design by Brittany Osborn

Published by Redemption Press, PO Box 427, Enumclaw, WA 98022
Toll Free (844) 2REDEEM (273-3336)

Redemption Press is honored to present this title in partnership with the author. The views expressed or implied in this work are those of the author. Redemption Press provides our imprint seal representing design excellence, creative content and high quality production.

Unless otherwise noted, Scriptures are taken from the *Holy Bible, New International Version®*, NIV®. Copyright © 1973, 1978, 1984, 2011 by Biblica, Inc.™ Used by permission of Zondervan. All rights reserved worldwide.

Scripture references marked KJV are taken from the *King James Version* of the Bible.

Scripture references marked ASV are taken from the *American Standard Version* of the Bible.

Stock Photos Purchased from: www.shutterstock.com
Credit/Attribution for Print: © Shutterstock / pranodhm
Designer: Brittany Osborn

ISBN 13: 978-1-68314-071-9
Library of Congress Catalog Card Number: 2016945737

CONTENTS

INTRODUCTION

THROUGH JESUS CHRIST, you can find forgiveness for your sins. In most religions you are told that if your good deeds outweigh your bad deeds, God will accept you into heaven when you die. But there is no way to get forgiven.

My wife once made a tuna casserole using old tuna mixed in with new tuna. She used lots of noodles and fresh vegetables. The old tuna was too old, and it ruined the entire casserole. Not even the cat would taste it! It had a terrible smell. We had to throw the entire thing out. That's what it's like to have even a little sin mixed in with your good deeds. Your sin will cause you to suffer the judgment of God unless you find forgiveness.

God made a way for you to be forgiven and cleansed of sin. He came himself in the form of man. Jesus Christ is the everlasting Word of God made flesh. God is one God but consists of three persons: Father, Son, and Holy Spirit. They are in each other and cannot be separated. They do everything together and never act independently. So there is *one* God.

God took upon himself the form of man, and this man was and is Jesus Christ. Because "all the fullness of deity lives in

Jesus in bodily form" (Col. 2:9), that means infinite goodness was in Jesus. When he willingly died on the cross for your sins, infinite goodness died in the place of trillions of human sins. Because he was God in human form, the sacrifice of his life and his shed blood paid the penalty for your sin and mine. He had no sin, so his sacrifice of infinite goodness provided a way for you to be forgiven for your sins.

Now, through Christ, you don't have to mix good deeds in with your sin and hope that your life won't have the bad odor of sin when you stand before the judgment throne of God.

God placed all the sin of the world on one side of a balance scale and put the goodness of Jesus Christ on the other side of the scale. The goodness of Jesus far outweighed all the sins of the human race. If Jesus were not God in human form, his sacrifice would not have been enough. To prove that he was indeed the Son of God or God in human form, he rose from the dead and appeared to his disciples over a forty-day period before ascending into heaven.

When you believe that Jesus is God's anointed one, the Christ, the Messiah—the answer to our sin problem—then you must receive him into your life. "To as many as received him, to them gave the power to become the sons of God" (John 1:12). The Greek word for sons in the original manuscript means "adult or full grown sons." God's free gift in Christ is forgiveness for sin and also power to become a full grown child of God.

Jesus Christ is the great forgiver. Although he healed all who were sick and performed many signs and miracles, the religious leaders of his day had him put to death by crucifixion. He could have resisted this by calling twelve legions of angels to his assistance (Matt. 26:53–54), but he allowed his own death to happen so that the shedding of his holy blood could pay the price for your salvation.

On the cross, as he was dying, Jesus said, "Father, forgive them; for they know not what they do" (Luke 23:34 KJV).

Come to Christ. Tell God that you believe Jesus is the Son of God—God in human form. Tell God that you do not want to live in sin. Tell God that you want to be a true child of his. Tell God you are truly sorry for the sins you have committed and then ask for his forgiveness.

Receive forgiveness for your sins and the free gift of eternal life—the power to become a full grown child of God. Now, thank God that you are forgiven. Thank God that Jesus Christ has become your righteousness.

Sometimes people tell me, "I just cannot forgive myself." This is a misnomer. You don't really forgive yourself. If you have been forgiven by almighty God, then you don't need any more forgiveness. You have all there is. What people really mean and ought to say is, "I keep letting the devil condemn me for sins God has forgiven. By listening to Satan's accusations, I'm allowing myself to feel condemned and guilty for things God has forgiven and forgotten." That would be an accurate statement. If you are one who says, "I'm not able to forgive myself," just change your confession. Learn to say, "Almighty God has forgiven me. I'm forgiven and God has forgotten about it. I'm free from condemnation thanks to the grace of God in Christ Jesus. Therefore, I resist Satan's efforts to remind me of past sins. I rebuke the "accuser of the brethren" in Jesus name! I will not listen to his condemning voice."

Next, learn to forgive others. Jesus taught that if we refuse to forgive others, we will forfeit or lose the gift of forgiveness for our own sins. Therefore, it is of utmost importance that we forgive those who have sinned against us.

Jesus taught us to pray, "Forgive us our debts as we forgive our debtors" (Matt. 6:12 KJV).

Over the many years of my Christian life, God has taught me twenty-one different ways to forgive. Sometimes everything I knew about forgiveness didn't seem quite enough. That's when the Holy Spirit taught me yet another way to forgive.

This little booklet was written to help you learn those twenty-one ways to forgive so that you can be certain that you have forgiven others from your heart. Some of these ways will help you completely avoid having any registered offense to forgive. For instance, if you overlook an offense you'll never have to forgive it. Other ways will help you actually forgive from the heart. Different situations may require different techniques. The remaining "ways to forgive" will actually help you clear away the rubble of sadness, self-pity, sorrow and victim mentality. But first, here are nine reasons why we *must* forgive others.

PART 1

WHY WE MUST FORGIVE

WE FORGIVE SO WE DON'T GO TO HELL

N O ONE IS worth going to hell over. Say that aloud to yourself: "No one is worth going to hell over." Jesus taught that if we refuse to forgive, that choice forfeits our own forgiveness. If a "Christian" died with real unforgiveness in his or her heart, it would be a form of rebellion against God. The blood of Christ does not cover rebellion and idolatry. The result would be a loss of salvation.

Unless you forgive, you'll end up here.

Then Peter came to Jesus and asked, "Lord, how many times shall I forgive my brother when he sins against me? Up to seven times?" Jesus answered, "I tell you, not seven times, but seventy-seven times. Therefore, the kingdom of heaven is like a king who wanted to settle accounts with his servants. As he began the settlement, a man who owed him ten thousand bags of gold was brought to him. Since he was not able to pay, the master ordered that he and his wife and his children and all that he had be sold to repay the debt. The servant fell on his knees before him. 'Be patient with me,' he begged, 'and I will pay back everything.' The servant's master took pity on him, canceled the debt and let him go. But when that servant went out, he found one of his fellow servants who owed him a hundred silver coins. He grabbed him and began to choke him. 'Pay back what you owe me!' he demanded. His fellow servant fell to his knees and begged him, 'Be patient with me, and I will pay you back.' But he refused. Instead, he went off and had the man thrown into prison until he could pay the debt. When the other servants saw what had happened, they were greatly distressed and went and told their master everything that had happened. Then the master called the servant in. 'You wicked servant,' he said, 'I canceled all that debt of yours because you begged me to. Shouldn't you have had mercy on your fellow servant just as I had on you?' In anger his master turned him over to the jailers to be tortured, until he should pay back all he owed. *This is how my heavenly Father will treat each of you unless you forgive your brother or sister from your heart.*"

(Matt. 18:21–35 emphasis added)

We need to make sure we've really forgiven from the heart. We don't want to have to pay our debt and be given over to the tormenters—evil spirits. Notice, in this parable the man was turned over to the jailers to be tortured until he paid back the entire debt. But of course, if he could not pay it back before going to jail, how much less could he pay it back from inside the jail? The meaning is, he would be tormented forever.

Make sure you get the point here. If you don't forgive from your heart, you'll pay the full penalty for your own sins in eternal punishment. That's a motivating thought!

WE FORGIVE SO THE DEVIL WON'T GET A FOOTHOLD IN OUR LIVES

PAUL WROTE, "IN your anger do not sin: Do not let the sun go down while you are still angry, and do not give the devil a foothold" (Eph. 4:26–27).

Holding onto anger gives the devil a foothold.

If you want to continue in a certain sin, the evil spirit behind that sin has a legal right to oppress you. If you hunger and thirst for righteousness, then the Holy Spirit, the source of all righteousness, has a legal right to bless you (Matt. 5:6). Blessed or oppressed? It's your choice.

If you refuse to forgive, you are giving the devil a legal right to oppress you. That oppression could come in many ways: depression, inner urgings to hurt other people, and possibly even suicide. The stress from bitterness, anger, hatred, and self-pity takes a terrible toll on physical and mental health and could result in lowering your immunity or raising your blood pressure to the point of increasing your risk for heart disease, cancer, and many other ailments.

The devil comes to steal, kill, and destroy (John 10:10), so any foothold you give him will only help him steal from you, kill you, or destroy you.

WE FORGIVE SO THE DEVIL WON'T OUTSMART US

Satan can only rule over the Unforgiven.

His scheme is to get you to not forgive so that he can brand you Unforgiven.

PAUL WROTE, "ANYONE you forgive, I also forgive. And what I have forgiven—if there was anything to forgive—I have forgiven in the sight of Christ for your sake, in order that Satan might not outwit us. For we are not unaware of his schemes" (2 Cor. 2:10–11).

Satan schemes to get you into a state of bitterness and unforgiveness toward others so that you cannot receive forgiveness from God. By getting you to be unforgiving of others, he can brand you "unforgiven." Then he can rule over you and destroy you.

Years ago I was in line at an amusement park and a teenager in front of me was wearing a T-shirt that advertised a famous rock music group. It showed a demon branding people "unforgiven" with a long line of these branded ones descending into hell. The caption read, "I dub thee unforgiven." I asked that young man if he had any idea what he was wearing. He was surprised when I told him that he had become a walking billboard advertising Satan's favorite scheme.

WE FORGIVE SO THAT OUR FAITH WILL WORK

"I command you to move!"   "Okay, I will."

If you don't get rid of your internal problems,
your external problems will pound you to pieces.

JESUS SAID, "HAVE faith in God. Truly I tell you, if anyone says to this mountain, 'Go, throw yourself into the sea,' and does not doubt in his heart but believes that what they say will happen, it will be done for them. Therefore, I tell you, whatever you ask for in prayer, believe that you have received it, and it will be yours. And when you stand praying, if you hold anything against anyone, forgive them, so that your Father in heaven may forgive you your sins" (Mark 11:22–26).

If we get rid of internal problems (heart issues), God will turn our external problems into blessings and miracles. If we don't forgive, we have an internal problem that will prevent our external problems from converting to miracles. Mountains won't move. If they do, they'll move over on top of us! A bitter, unforgiving person will be crushed by the external problems of life.

If you want your faith to be truly mountain-moving, then remember that forgiving others is a must.

WE FORGIVE SO OUR BITTERNESS WON'T DEFILE MANY OTHERS

Don't infect others with bitterness!

THE BIBLE SAYS, "See to it that no one falls short of the grace of God and that no bitter root grows up to cause trouble and defile many" (Heb. 12:15).

Bitterness can invade a family and spread from person to person like a virus. It's infectious like a disease. If you don't conquer it, you'll spread it. Then, even if you recover, some of the people who caught bitterness from you may not. Don't put your family at risk! Don't put your children at risk! Don't put your friends or co-workers at risk!

If you had the common cold and you were coughing, as an adult you'd know to cover your mouth when you cough. In the same way, if you are bitter, cover your mouth! Don't speak it and spread it to others. Instead, get alone with God, and the Holy Spirit will give you the thoughts and the grace to conquer it and be spiritually whole.

WE FORGIVE SO WE DON'T DIE OF STRESS-RELATED DISEASES

Don't let bitterness kill you.

NEGATIVE EMOTIONS TEAR up the human body. The Bible says, "Resentment kills a fool, and envy slays the simple" (Job 5:2). Solomon wrote, "A heart at peace gives life to the body, but envy rots the bones" (Prov. 14:30).

In my own life, I've found that every time I thought strong negative thoughts for three straight days, I would catch a terrible cold. Remember, the Israelites who were in the desert with Moses were eating the best health food—manna, the food of angels. Manna had every vitamin, mineral, pro-biotic, and enzyme needed for health. Yet almost all of that generation died prematurely because of their terrible unbelief, grumbling, complaining, and negativity.

The number-one health concept is to have loving, kind, and peaceful thoughts that give life to your body. We must forgive to avoid an early grave. Who wants to be buried in Negative Emotions Memorial Garden?

WE FORGIVE BECAUSE WE WANT TO BE LIKE JESUS AND HAVE COMPLETE INTIMACY WITH THE FATHER

Don't let bitterness wreck your glorious fellowship with God.

DO YOU WANT to be like Jesus? Jesus prayed, "I have given them the glory that you gave me, that they may be one as we are one—I in them and you in me—so that they may be brought to complete unity. Then the world will know that you sent me and have loved them even as you have loved me" (John 17:22–23).

This is the ultimate gift. Jesus wants you to have the same intimate oneness that he has with the Father. This is glorious intimacy with almighty God. It is available through Jesus Christ because the Holy Spirit, whom he sent to us, leads us into all truth and counsels us how to walk and live like Jesus.

Unforgiveness against people breaks our fellowship with God. We also know that unforgiveness breaks fellowship with people. Jesus said, "Love the Lord your God with all your heart and with all your soul and with all your mind. This is the first and greatest commandment. And the second is like it: Love your neighbor as yourself" (Matt. 22:37–39). When you love people and show kindness to them, God takes it personally as if the kindness was shown directly to him. When you hate people, abuse them, or neglect them, God takes that personally as if you failed to love him.

Anger and revenge are, of course, the opposite of loving your neighbor and the opposite of loving your enemy. We must forgive so that bitterness doesn't rob us of the greatest gift of all, intimacy with God.

WE FORGIVE SO WE WON'T DO SOMETHING REALLY EVIL

**Don't nurse a grudge!
It will grow into something murderous!**

ARK RECORDS, "SO Herodias nursed a grudge against John and wanted to kill him" (Mark 6:19). Herodias divorced her husband and married her brother-in-law, King Herod. The prophet John the Baptist rebuked Herodias and King Herod for this adulterous marriage. Instead of getting rid of her sin in repentance, she decided to get rid of the messenger. When her daughter danced for King Herod and pleased him, he promised to give her anything she asked for up to half of his kingdom. Her mother, Herodias, counseled her to ask for the head of John the Baptist, so this wonderful man of God was murdered.

Likewise, if you nurse a little baby monster, it will grow into a big dangerous monster. Don't nurse a little grudge. It may grow into something really terrible. The grudge Herodias nursed grew into the monstrous sin of murder. Are you nursing a grudge? Remember, if you do, it will *not* stay a little grudge. It will grow and eventually be terribly dangerous and destructive to others and to you.

WE FORGIVE TO BE SUCCESSFUL IN LIFE

Success without peace of mind is *not* success. Forgive!

Peace of mind is success. Forgive!

THERE ARE MANY definitions of what success is. UCLA head basketball coach John Wooden said, "Success is peace of mind, which is a direct result of self-satisfaction in knowing you did your best to become the best that you were capable of becoming." Simply put: success is peace of mind. There can be no peace of mind when we haven't forgiven someone or when we dwell in sadness because we are focused on the bad things people did to us. To be successful, we must clean the slate of past offenses and move on. The Psalmist wrote, "Great peace have they which love thy law: and nothing shall offend them" (Ps. 119:165 KJV).

It doesn't matter if you win award after award, trophy after trophy, or medal after medal. If you have no peace of mind, you are not a champion. You are only a true success in life if your life is filled with the peace of God.

There are probably reasons without number as to why we should forgive. Innumerable good things will happen if we forgive and innumerable bad things will happen if we do not forgive. It is most important to remember: your salvation is at stake!

PART 2

TOOLS AND TECHNIQUES OF FORGIVENESS

CONSTRUCTION IS A word that involves the use of many different tools. Likewise, forgiveness happens through the use of various techniques or what I call tools of forgiveness. I've learned twenty-one different ways to forgive. Sometimes everything I knew already wasn't enough to get forgiveness completed. Whenever that happened God was gracious to show me some new technique.

If you take these to heart and practice them, you can avoid bitterness, rage, anger, self-pity, and sadness. If you are already suffering from these negative emotions, you can use these biblical methods to get spiritually clean and free. You can get back to peace of mind and heart.

Please make a note of this: forgiveness and trust are two different things. Forgiveness is freely given. Trust must be earned. This book will help you forgive people. How the people you forgive rebuild trust is another subject not covered in this book. Similarly, this book does not discuss the issue of justice. If a thief steals your property, of course you'll want justice. If someone murdered a family member, you would want that person to be arrested and proven guilty. Trust, justice and forgiveness are not enemies of each other. They don't negate each other. The purpose of this book is to help you with forgiveness, and its small size precludes a full discussion of the issues of trust and justice.

If you forgive, you don't have to throw the desire for justice out the window. If you forgive, you do not have to immediately trust the person you forgave. They'll have to earn back your trust. In criminal cases, justice should be pursued.

Suppose someone said, "Now that you've forgiven me for embezzling all of your pension fund, I'd like my job of being your bookkeeper back again. Unless you rehire me, you haven't forgiven me." If something like that were to happen, you should say, "Forgiveness is free. Trust must be earned." The Holy Spirit will coach you if you ask for his help. He can give you a plan whereby people can regain your trust by earning it again. However, if a pedophile sexually abused several children and was forgiven, it would not be wise to ever trust that person to oversee a church nursery or babysit your young children. Still, you would want to avoid hating that person and dying with a bitter unforgiving heart toward them. Here, then, are twenty-one ways to forgive.

OVERLOOK IT. BLOW IT OFF. PAY NO ATTENTION TO IT

THE BIBLE SAYS, "A person's wisdom yields patience; it is to one's glory to overlook an offense" (Prov. 19:11).

This applies in smaller things. If someone murders a family member or friend, you can't overlook that. However, if someone insults you or is rude to you, then you do not have to take offense. Just act as though it didn't happen, as if you didn't see or hear it. Don't record it.

A similar verse reads, "It is to one's honor to avoid strife, but every fool is quick to quarrel" (Prov. 20:3). The fool thinks he is defending his honor when he is, in fact, losing it by getting into strife. Keep your spiritual dignity. No one can take it from you. I've heard angry people say, "I'm going to give that person a piece of my mind!" Don't give someone a piece of your mind when you need all the pieces yourself.

Imagine a five-gallon can of water filled to the brim. If a burning ember from a forest fire blew into that open can of water, what would happen? The ember would be extinguished.

What will happen? **Nothing.**

burning ember

H²O

If a burning ember falls into an open can of gasoline, what will happen?

GAS

Now imagine a five-gallon can of gasoline filled to the brim. If a burning ember from a forest fire fell into that can, what would happen? It would explode!

Suppose a burning ember of offense blows into your life, and you explode in anger. Should you blame it on the burning ember? Isn't the real cause of your explosion the fact that you are filled with a spiritual form of gasoline—pride, self-pity, and impatience?

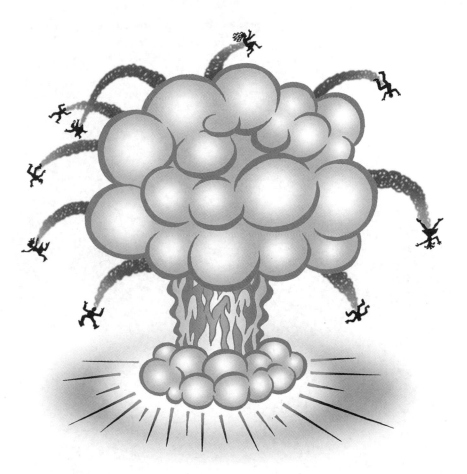

This is why it's a form of self-deception to say, "She made me angry! I blew up in anger because of her terribly offensive remarks." No, if you were full of living water from the Holy Spirit, the offense would have simply gone out. So ask God to fill you with humility, patience, and wisdom, and you'll be able to overlook many offenses. You'll never even get to the point where you have to forgive it because you overlooked it in the beginning.

2

DROP THE MATTER

THE BIBLE SAYS, "Starting a quarrel is like breaching a dam; so drop the matter before a dispute breaks out" (Prov. 17:14).

Suppose a foolish man was angry with the Hoover Dam, which forms one of the greatest man-made lakes in the world. Imagine that this man stood down below the dam and detonated an explosive that blew up the dam. He would destroy the dam he hated but he, himself, would be washed away in the breakout of floodwaters.

That's what it's like when you choose to keep a quarrel going. You might breach the dam and be destroyed in the resulting dispute.

A quarrel usually starts when you respond in anger to someone who you perceive has wronged

27

you. Sometimes when I'm driving a car at night another driver will drive close behind my car with their bright lights on. This is very irritating, needless to say. Probably the person just isn't thinking what they are doing and means no harm. But if I pull over, let that car pass, and then drive up behind them with my lights on bright to show them what it felt like, that wrong response is "starting a quarrel."

Who knows? The person might be on drugs. They might be on some antidepressant medicine that makes people more prone to kill others. The person might have a gun. So if I catch myself on the verge of showing them what it felt like, I quote Proverbs 17:14, "Starting a quarrel is like breaching a dam; so drop the matter before a dispute breaks out." I drop the matter.

Recently I wanted to buy light bulbs. The carton of four bulbs contained one broken bulb. I told the clerk I would buy the package if they discounted it for the one broken bulb. She called the manager who set a lower price off the top of his head without doing the math of taking 25 percent off. I thought that sounded too high, so I got a paper and pen and found he had over charged me by twelve cents.

This clerk had to call the manager back, and I explained that I did the math and that the price should be $3.88, not the $4 he had said. To my surprise he said, "Then we'll keep it." He turned his back and walked away.

For just twelve cents, he was willing to lose a good customer. I thought about writing a negative review on the Internet. I pondered getting the corporate address of the company and writing a complaint. I thought for a while I'd never shop at that store again. However, it's a good store and very close to my house.

While his customer service leaves a lot to be desired, I've decided to just drop the matter. Why go to war over twelve cents?

3

USE THE SHIELD OF BLESSING

Be quick to bless those who curse you.

ETER WROTE, "DO not repay evil with evil or insult with insult. On the contrary, repay evil with blessing, because to this you were called so that you may inherit a blessing" (1 Peter 3:9).

Zig Ziglar was a famous salesman and motivational speaker. One day as he pulled his car up to a stop sign, he drove a bit too far out into the road, and the passing motorist swerved to avoid hitting him. That man, who was driving a convertible, immediately swore at Zig and gave him an obscene gesture. Immediately Zig waved vigorously and yelled, "Hi friend." The other guy waved back, thinking he had insulted one of his friends!

The Apostle Paul wrote, "When we are cursed, we bless. When we are persecuted, we endure it; when we are slandered, we answer kindly," (1 Cor. 4:11-12). The idea is to become mature in Christ so that when cursed we have a spiritual reflex that immediately blesses. Then we don't have to brood for days and finally decide to forgive.

If you want to inherit a blessing, then never return an insult for an insult. Insults for insults result in the growth of bitterness and unforgiveness. If you avoid getting bitter in the first place, then you won't have to get over bitterness. Best of all, if you bless those who curse you, you will inherit a blessing. It's God's guarantee.

4

BEAR WITH ONE ANOTHER

PEOPLE AREN'T PERFECT so don't require them to be. Don't make them walk on eggshells when they are around you.

An expression I've heard is, "He wears his feelings on his shirtsleeves." In other words, that person was very easy to offend. Don't wear your feelings on your shirtsleeves.

Paul taught us, "Bear with each other and forgive one another if any of you has a grievance against someone. Forgive as the Lord forgave you" (Col. 3:13).

If you forgive as the Lord forgave you, then you must forget about it. God forgets when he forgives. Don't reach into the slime bag of the past to get a wad of slimy, bitter memories in order to smear it all over today! You can ruin each today if you smear it with some slime you've been holding onto for years. Some people have a huge collection of grievances they keep stored in their slime bag of the past. They keep it handy so that they can reach in and grab that slime and smear it all over each fresh new day. The longer a grievance stays in the slime bag of the past, the more rotten and stinky it will become!

Why slime today with the past?

EACH NEW DAY starts off beautiful. It's like a painting with a bright sun shining on a garden of beautiful grass, flowers, and trees. If nothing from the past is rubbed on today, then today will most likely be a pretty good day.

Suppose a wife keeps a bag of grievances in her heart. Suppose those grievances go back to the very beginning of her relationship with her husband. Each new day could be a pretty good day if she would refrain from reaching into that slime bag and rubbing the past all over today. Whether you are a wife or a husband, a sister or a brother, or a son or a daughter—if you want a good relationship with someone else, you need to *forget* what you forgive. "It [love] keeps no record of wrongs" (1 Cor. 13:5).

I went to grade school in a one-room schoolhouse. At the front of the classroom was a wall-to-wall chalkboard. The teacher would ask students to write spelling words or math equations on that board. At the end of every day, one child was assigned to wash the chalkboard using a pail of water and a sponge. That way, it was totally clean for the next day. An unwashed chalkboard would be useless the next day because of the build-up of written words and equations.

To bear with one another, you need to erase the chalkboard of your mind where the offenses were written down. Start each day with a clean chalkboard. Do you ever erase the bad things people do to you? You'll not be able to enjoy your family if you don't erase your chalkboard. A chalkboard that's never erased is useless. A mind where nothing is erased becomes a cluttered and messed up mind. The Bible urges us to clean our mental chalkboards at least once a day. "In your anger do not sin: Do not let the sun go down while you are still angry" (Eph. 4:26).

STOP FEEDING BITTERNESS WITH VERBAL HOSTILITY

ARDENING STORES SELL fertilizer products. One that I've used in gardening is called Miracle Grow. I would never put Miracle Grow on weeds or thistles. Verbal hostility is like a strong fertilizer that will cause bitterness to grow.

Here's an example of what I call a sweet spirit verse: "Do not let any unwholesome talk come out of your mouths, but only what is helpful for building others up according to their needs, that it may benefit those who listen" (Eph. 4:29).

If you try to make someone feel guilty and condemned and you succeed, they'll be looking down at themselves, thinking how bad they are. Then they can't possibly look up to see how good you are. Wouldn't you rather have them looking at you and thinking how good you are? If so, don't use condemnation to make them feel guilty.

Remember the story of the woman caught in adultery? Some teachers of the Law brought to Jesus a woman who was caught in the act of adultery. They said, "In the Law Moses commanded us to stone such women. Now what do you say?" Jesus just bent down and started to write on the ground with his finger. When they kept on questioning him, he straightened up and said to them, "Let any one of you who is without sin be the first to throw a stone at her." Again he stooped down and wrote on the ground, probably writing different sins the group of condemners had participated in themselves. One by one, starting with the oldest, they all left until Jesus and the woman were all alone.

Jesus said, "Woman, where are they? Has no one condemned you?"

"No one, sir," she said.

He said, "Then neither do I condemn you. Go now and leave your life of sin" (John 8:3–11).

That woman looked up at Jesus. She saw how wonderful he was. She left thinking how good he was; not how bad she had been. If he had condemned her, she would have left focused only on herself and her shame.

Some people, however, pour the strong fertilizer of verbal hostility upon those around them until a root of bitterness grows into a life-threatening monster. Will you be foolish like those people or wise and loving like Jesus?

6

FORGIVE AS A DECISION OF YOUR WILL

I T DOESN'T TAKE long to describe this method of forgiveness. It's like canceling a debt. You can forgive a debt if you want to. Forgiveness is like that. You do it because you can. In this method, you just decide to forgive as if you are cancelling a debt. It's as if you stamp the debt: *forgiven*. Jesus taught us to use this technique when we pray, "Forgive us our debts, as we also have forgiven our debtors" (Matt. 6:12).

If this works for your situation, then use this method because it's quick and easy. However, if you say you have forgiven someone, but what they did keeps coming to your mind and negative emotions keep flooding your soul, I urge you to combine several other methods with this one to make sure the forgiveness is total and from your heart.

7

ASK GOD TO FORGIVE THEM

I F THE OFFENSE is small to medium, you forgive it. Just handle it yourself. But if the wrong done to you is huge, ask God to forgive it. Remember that Jesus said to people on occasion, "Your sins are forgiven." He said that to a paralyzed man before he healed him (Matt. 9:2). He said those same words to the woman who washed his feet with her tears and dried them with her hair (Luke 7:48). To the woman taken in adultery he said, "Neither do I condemn you. Go now and leave your life of sin" (John 8:11).

But he did *not* say this to those who were crucifying him. Their sins were too great. Their sins were blasphemy, cruelty, mockery, torture, murder, and the greatest injustice in all of human history—murdering the Son of God. So Jesus asked the Father to forgive them. "Jesus said, 'Father, forgive them, for they do not know what they are doing.' And they divided up his clothes by casting lots" (Luke 23:34). Jesus died without any bitterness in his heart. He died completely sinless.

Small to Medium Offense = You Forgive It

If offense is huge, ask God to forgive it.

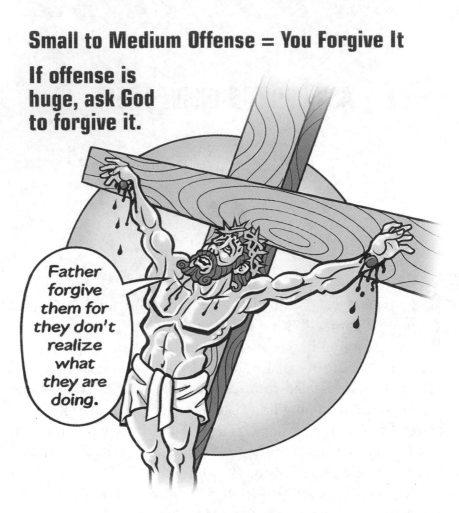

Have you suffered some huge injustice? Does it seem like such a crime that you aren't big enough to forgive it? If so, ask the Father, almighty God, to forgive it and be sincere.

Paul wrote, "I want to know Christ—yes, to know the power of his resurrection and participation in his sufferings, becoming like him in his death" (Phil. 3:10). We should desire to be like Jesus in life and in death. In death, Jesus died completely free of bitterness and unforgiveness because, although what was done to him was the greatest injustice in all of human history, he asked the Father to forgive them. You can do the same.

8

FORGIVE BEFORE THEY ASK FOR FORGIVENESS

JESUS SAID, "AND when you stand praying, if you hold anything against anyone, forgive them, so that your Father in heaven may forgive you your sins" (Mark 11:25–26).

When I was just twenty-three and in my first year in the ministry, a man hurled insults against me in front of about twenty people. When he didn't repent, I said in my heart, "He's a bigger turkey than I thought he was."

God convicted me. Then I said, "Father, don't you remember when Jesus said, 'If your brother or sister sins against you, rebuke them; and if they repent, forgive them?' (Luke 17:3). He hasn't repented. That's why I haven't forgiven him."

Immediately the Holy Spirit said, "You're just like a man that went to the beach. A seagull flew over his head and had a bowel movement that landed right on the man's nose. The man looked at the bird as it flew away and said, 'You dirty bird, you! I'm going to leave this right here on my face until you come back and wipe it off!'"

Then the Holy Spirit said, "Bitterness is showing on your face, and you can't hide it." I was stunned.

I asked, "How do I get it off?"

He said, "Forgive him before he asks."

I forgave that man with all my heart, although I never told him. But whenever I was around him there was no bitterness on my face. I was friendly as if nothing had ever happened. He never said that he was sorry, but he began to bring me presents of venison and homemade granola. We became friends.

Years later I became a lead pastor and birds flew over in herds. I was forgiving individuals and groups of people so often it was as if I was saying "I forgive them, I forgive them, I forgive them," non-stop.

Then one day God sent a messenger to tell me, "God says you are holding on to something in one of your hands so that you can only work for God with one hand. He wants you to let go of what you are holding on to so you can work with both hands."

I didn't like that corrective word. So later that day, I asked God if there was anything to that message. I asked, "Am I holding on to something in one of my hands?"

God said, "Yes."

I was very surprised! "What is it, Father?"

He said, "It's what you wiped off your face."

I was forgiving, but not forgetting. So I was holding onto what I had forgiven. I wiped bitterness off of my face, but I was holding self-pity in my hand! Often I'd review the mean things people had done to me. Then I'd say, "But I forgave her." I'd review another injustice and say, "But I forgave him." I'd review what a group of people did to me. Then I'd say, "But I forgave them." Finally, I'd say, "Oh God, has any pastor ever been so mistreated in the history of the world?" I actually asked God that!

God taught me that a major part of forgiving is forgetting all about it. Let go of it so it doesn't turn into the bondage of self-pity. Paul wrote, "Therefore I want the men everywhere to pray, lifting up holy hands without anger and disputing" (1 Tim. 2:8). Wipe the bird stuff off of your nose and say, "I forgive them." Now dust your hands together and say, "I'm going to let it go and forget about it. I will not hold on to self-pity!" Now lift up holy hands to God in praise.

9

FEEL SORRY FOR THEM, NOT YOURSELF

Response of the Immature Christian

Response of the Mature Christian

O NE DAY I recognized I was allowing myself to wallow in self-pity. I was driving a car and had stopped at a red light. Before the light turned green, I wrote a short poem. It went like this:

I've been slowly dying of sorry for me
It hurts really bad, but I want to be free.
The Bible I love and know to be true
Says I'll soon feel much better—feeling sorry for you!

Mature people feel sorry for those who do wrong to them. Immature people feel sorry for themselves. The apostle Paul is a fine example of a mature person feeling sorry for his oppressors instead of himself.

"Five times I received from the Jews the forty lashes minus one. Three times I was beaten with rods, once I was pelted with stones . . ." (2 Cor. 11:24–25).

"I speak the truth in Christ—I am not lying, my conscience confirms it through the Holy Spirit—I have great sorrow and unceasing anguish in my heart. For I could wish that I myself were cursed and cut off from Christ for the sake of my people, those of my own race, the people of Israel" (Rom. 9:1–4).

Paul was saying, "If I could exchange my soul for theirs I would be willing to be lost and suffer for eternity so that they could be saved." No one can actually do that, but there is no stronger way to say, "I love you." Paul did not feel great sorrow for himself. He felt great sorrow for those lost souls who had persecuted him.

When you feel sorry for yourself, you are a victim. But if you feel sorry for the person or people who victimized you, that moves you from victim status to being more than a conqueror in Christ Jesus.

If you are currently in an abusive relationship or situation I am not saying that you must stay in that situation and merely feel sorry for your abuser. God understands that there are situations that require getting away from the abuser.

Malachi 2:16 Amplified says, "For I hate divorce, says the Lord, the God of Israel, and him who covers his garment with wrong and violence, says the Lord of hosts." God hates divorce but he also hates what causes divorce and domestic violence is one of those things. If you think you are putting up with too much please seek the counsel of wise spiritual people. God doesn't want you to be a punching bag or a doormat.

10

INVEST YOUR PAIN IN THE BANK OF HEAVEN

ACTS 7:60 SAYS, "Then he fell on his knees and cried out, 'Lord, do not hold this sin against them.' When he had said this, he fell asleep."

When Stephen was being stoned, Saul of Tarsus was the focal point of the guilt. He was the man of authority, holding the coats of those who threw the stones. He wasn't a boy; he was a Sanhedrin member and the whole event was happening under his authority, sanctioned and promoted by him! That made him the focal point of the guilt.

When Stephen said, "Lord, do not hold this sin against them," he was, in essence, investing his pain in the bank of heaven. God used this invested pain of Stephen as a legal means of revealing himself in mercy to Saul instead of revealing himself to Saul in judgment. Saul became the focal point of divine mercy.

When Saul was on a trip to Damascus to jail and persecute more Christians, a lightning bolt of divine mercy struck him to the ground. He was changed from a persecutor of Christians into an apostle, a "sent one" who eventually wrote thirteen books of the Bible. He became, arguably, the most fruitful of all the apostles.

When you forgive, God doesn't brush your pain into a wastebasket and take it to the trash dumpster. Rather, your pain is invested, like a treasure, in the bank of heaven. There it gives God a legal right to reveal himself to those people who hurt you, who most likely are not seeking to know God.

If you are familiar with network marketing, you know that it's very profitable to sign up someone who will then sign up multitudes of others. You will get paid some amount of money on all of them. Stephen got the apostle Paul in his spiritual down-line. He gets a percentage of all Paul's rewards. What a great investment on his pain, suffering, and ultimate martyrdom.

One of my dear friends is a pastor. In a vision, he saw three men shaking their fingers at him and saying bad things about him. In the vision, God cut the ends of their pointing fingers off at the first joint. This began to actually happen in real life. One man cut the end of his finger off in a lawn mower accident. The next week another one of those men cut the end of his finger off in a hedge trimmer accident.

My pastor friend phoned the third man, told him the vision, and then said, "You are going to lose the end of your finger too if you don't repent." That man drove to the church and repented to the pastor. God let him keep the end of his finger.

Thinking about this, I said to God, "Those men didn't do *anything* to my friend compared to what these people did to me. Don't you think you should cut their heads off?"

That's when God showed me that if he took my pain and struck them with a lightning bolt of divine justice, I'd only have a pool of blood or a big grease spot to show where they'd been burned up. But if he took my pain and used it as a legal justification to strike them with mercy, I might get a righteous man or even an apostle as a result!

God asked me, "Would you rather have a grease spot or an apostle?"

I said, "I'd rather have an apostle." So I committed all my pain into the bank of heaven and asked with all my heart that God would use my pain as a legal justification to strike those who had hurt me with bolts of divine mercy and turn them into wonderful, fruit-bearing disciples.

In many nations of the world, Christians are viciously persecuted. Yet the more they are persecuted, the faster the church grows. How can that be? I believe this principle is behind that phenomenon. As Christians forgive those who have persecuted them they are in fact investing their pain in the bank of heaven. They give God a legal right to reveal himself in mercy to those people. Many of these persecutors end up having dreams or visions of Jesus and become powerful fully dedicated Christians. Remember, God will never waste your pain if you will invest it in the bank of heaven.

Someone might ask, "How do I forgive someone who is already dead?" I'd suggest using this technique. The Bible says, "Yet he does not leave the guilty unpunished; he punishes the children and their children for the sin of the parents to the third and fourth generation" (Exodus 34:7). If the person who caused you great pain is dead, why not tell God that you'd still like to invest your pain in the bank of heaven? Tell God that you'd really like him to strike the *descendants* of the person who harmed you with bolts of mercy if at all possible, and turn them into righteous people.

11

TAKE THE STEPS OUT OF SADNESS

SUPPOSE THAT WE could be sad for a lot of reasons or perhaps sad at our own failures. But usually we are sad because of what someone has done to us or not done for us. Our focus is, "I'm so sad. Look what they did to me!" When you are focused on what others did wrong to you, you will be sad, and you'll stay sad until you change that focus. We can choose to move out of sadness because we can change what we are focused on. When I was very sad because of a huge church split I endured, God taught me to take these steps out of sadness.

What Sadness Looks Like

I'm SO sad. Look what they did to me!

Step 1: Say this, "That was just the devil. I can't expect the devil to be good." Paul wrote, "For we wrestle not against flesh and blood, but against principalities, against powers, against the rulers of darkness of this world, against spiritual wickedness in high places" (Eph. 6:12 KJV). The devil used people as if they were puppets. He's the one who caused you so much trouble. The devil is behind every mean and bad thing anyone has done to you. He's your real enemy, and he's not going to change or become nice.

Step 2: Say this, "I'm still alive. I can counterattack the devil." It's all right to be angry at the devil. He is our enemy. Paul wrote, "The God of peace will soon crush Satan under your feet" (Rom. 16:20). Quit fighting flesh (people) as if they were your enemy. Your real enemy is an unseen, spiritual enemy.

Step 3: Say this, "I'll counterattack the devil by helping people. Who can I help?" It is extremely important that you counterattack the devil by helping people. Don't shout at the devil. Don't try to bind spiritual evil forces in the

heavenly realms. That's called *unscriptural binding*. Jesus said, "Whatever you bind on earth will be bound in heaven" (Matt. 16:19). You may have to bind some demon on earth, but God will take care of the evil angels in the second heaven. Never be shouting up at the devil! Positionally, God has placed the devil beneath our feet! We are in Christ. We are his body. "God has put everything under his feet" (1 Cor. 15:27).

CISTERN of SADNESS

I'll counterattack the devil by helping people. Who can I help?

Steps Out Of Sadness

Step #3

You will read some books on deliverance that tell you to bind spiritual forces in the heavenlies so that revival will break out on earth. I tell you, that is wrong! It will summon demons down upon you! Demons will manifest on those you pray for. You will think everyone has demons because you'll be summoning demons and not even know it!

The Muslim religion has a special day where people gather in Mecca, Saudi Arabia, and throw stones at stone pillars that represent the devil. Almost every time they do this, there is some huge disturbance in the crowd and scores or even hundreds of people are trampled to death. This is because throwing stones at the devil glorifies the devil in his perverted mind. It gives him attention. He views it as worship. So he comes to that, and when he comes, he brings death!

God taught me: "Major on worship. Minor on warfare. Major on revealing Christ. Minor on exposing the devil." So when it comes to counterattacking the devil, just go help hurting, suffering people! Show love to people. That's the best way to destroy the devil's kingdom.

Step 4: After you devote yourself to helping people, you'll be able to look back and say, "I'm so happy. Look how God used me to help other people!" Once that happens, you are completely out of what I call the Cistern of Sadness.

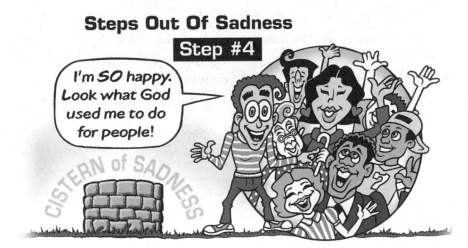

Remember, after you help a bunch of people, you'll look back on what good you did for others instead of looking back on the bad others did to you. This is the difference between those who are glad and those who are sad.

Certain sins done against us are big enough to dominate our minds for days, weeks, years, and even for the rest of our lives. When that is happening, we must put a stop to it. These four steps work!

In 1996, I went through a terrible church split before becoming an evangelist. In January of 1997, I began to travel as a teacher/evangelist. I held revival/seminars in churches and would pray for people to be baptized in the Holy Spirit. In 1997, two hundred people were baptized in the Holy Spirit in my meetings. That was more than had been baptized in the Holy Spirit during my fifteen years of pastoral ministry. Since then, thousands have been baptized in the Holy Spirit in my meetings. I can barely remember the big church split, and if I think of it, there is absolutely no pain. Instead, I think of all the wonderful fruit I've seen since then: miraculous healings, people being saved, books written and published, and thousands getting baptized in the Holy Spirit.

I'm happy. My focus in life is: Look how God has used me to love and minister to many people! I'm delighted rather than sad. The church split isn't the last time someone has hurt me or done bad things to me. But in each new trial, I avoid falling back into the Cistern of Sadness by immediately taking these four steps. You can too!

TELL GOD, "I DON'T WANT THEM TO GO TO HELL FOR WHAT THEY DID TO ME"

I do *not* want them to go to hell for what they did to me.

THIS IS ANOTHER way of saying Stephen's prayer, "Do not hold this sin against them" (Acts 7:60).

I've often used this technique as a beginning tool to break apart the bondage of bitterness. In one church I prayed for a couple whose marriage was in serious trouble. The man had committed adultery. He was terribly sorry and had broken off the affair. He wanted to save his marriage. The wife wanted to save the marriage as well, but she could not forgive him. She was crying profusely.

I said to her, "Do you want him to burn forever in hell because of what he did to you?"

She sobbed, "No. I don't want him to go to hell for what he did to me."

I said, "Then tell that to God. That's the beginning of forgiveness."

She cried as she said, "God, I don't want him to go to hell for what he did to me."

Then I was able to pray over them, and very soon she was able to lean into her husband and accept his embrace again.

I've heard people relate the most heart-wrenching stories of verbal, physical, sexual, and even satanic ritual abuse. Using this technique, I've helped many hundreds move out of bitterness into forgiveness, even in the most extreme cases. Telling God that you don't want a person to go to hell for what they did to you drives a wedge into the wall of unforgiveness and bitterness and begins to break it apart. As the bondage of bitterness crumbles into rubble, use some of these other techniques to clean up any mess that remains.

13

MAYBE THEY'LL LOVE YOU
MORE THAN EVER

**Forgive: They may end up
loving you more than anyone.**

WHEN YOU FORGIVE, Satan will tell you that it's stupid, that it makes no sense! But actually, it makes very good sense. The person who has been forgiven the very most is the person who is likely to love you the very most. Jesus made this very clear in Luke 7, beginning at verse 37:

A woman in that town who had lived a sinful life learned that Jesus was eating at the Pharisee's house, she brought an alabaster jar of perfume. As she stood behind him at his feet weeping, she began to wet his feet with her tears. Then she wiped them with her hair, kissed them and poured perfume on them.

When the Pharisee who had invited him saw this, he said to himself, "If this man were a prophet, he would know who is touching him and what kind of woman she is—that she is a sinner."

Jesus answered him, "Simon, I have something to tell you."

"Tell me, teacher," he said.

"Two men owed money to a certain moneylender. One owed him five hundred denarii, and the other fifty. Neither of them had the money to pay him back, so he forgave the debts of both. Now which of them will love him more?"

Simon replied, "I suppose the one who had the bigger debt forgiven."

"You have judged correctly," Jesus said. Then he turned toward the woman and said to Simon, "Do you see this woman? I came into your house. You did not give me any water for my feet, but she wet my feet with her tears and wiped them with her hair. You did not give me a kiss, but this woman, from the time I entered, has not stopped kissing my feet. You did not put oil on my head, but she has poured perfume on my feet. Therefore, I tell you, her many sins have been forgiven—as her great love has shown. *But whoever has been forgiven little loves little."*

Then Jesus said to her, "Your sins are forgiven."

The other guests began to say among themselves, "Who is this who even forgives sins?"

Jesus said to the woman, "Your faith has saved you; go in peace" (Luke 7:37–50 emphasis added).

Jesus had already forgiven her earlier, and that is why she loved him so much. He had already delivered her from sin. But in this context, he was reminding her that she was forgiven. Sometimes people need to be reminded.

This woman had been very sinful. But because Jesus had forgiven her of more than most other sinners, she loved him the very most. It's not stupid to forgive. It's smart. Satan wants to tell you that you are crazy for forgiving.

Sometimes we wonder if we're crazy to forgive certain things. But remember, those who are forgiven much love much. Go ahead and forgive them. They'll probably end up loving you more than most other people.

14

LET GOD SHOW YOU WHAT THEY CAN BECOME

Saul of Tarsus Killed *God's Children*

SAUL OF TARSUS murdered God's children. In Acts 22:4, Paul said, "I persecuted the followers of this Way to their death, arresting both men and women and throwing them into prison." At his trial he said, "And when they were put to death I cast my vote against them" (Acts 26:10). Paul was responsible for killing more than just Stephen. He put to death many Christians! He didn't just murder God's *child*. He murdered God's *children*!

Forgiving someone for murdering your children is perhaps the most difficult of all things to forgive. How did God forgive the man who murdered not just one, but many of God's very own children? God looked through what Saul was and saw what he could become. He saw that Saul could become the spiritual father of a multitude. He saw that Saul could bear many more spiritual children for God if he was forgiven.

The murder of God's children was a huge sin, yet God forgave Saul and turned him into an anointed apostle. As Christ's sent-one, Paul bore many thousands of spiritual children for Christ. Through his writings that every soul winner around the world uses, we could say that Paul has born millions of spiritual children for God!

Once Forgiven, Saul - *The Apostle Paul* - Bore God Many *More* Spiritual Children

There are Christians in the world who have had terrorists or perverts murder their children. Could anything be more difficult to forgive? I hope you will never have to use this technique of forgiveness. I hope you will never experience the horror of having someone kill one of your loved ones.

But if, God forbid, you should ever experience the pain that comes from someone killing your very own child, children, or spouse, then see what the killer could become. If you forgive them, they could end up bearing you many more spiritual children. In heaven, when you meet the people they have won to Christ, it will be like meeting your very own descendants who came from your body. These children will have come from your pain.

What can they become if you forgive them? God knows. Ask him to show you. Dare to find out! Put all your pain into the bank of heaven and ask God to strike those who have hurt you with bolts of divine mercy.

Once when I was considering why God would allow Christians to be martyred, I felt God breath a thought into me, "We leverage our losses." This communication from God came very gently, like a breath from heaven. As I thought about it, I realized that God never just lets the devil give the Kingdom of God a defeat. If something appears to be a loss, like the loss of Stephen when he was stoned, then the Father, Son and Holy Spirit "leverage" that loss. They use it as a fulcrum, put a spiritual lever over it, and pry the kingdom of darkness out of its place.

When Stephen was killed and a great persecution of Christians began, the believers scattered to far places but went everywhere preaching the Word. (See Acts 8:4.) Thus, the loss was leveraged to a gain. God used Stephen's prayer, "Lord lay not this sin to their charge" to justify revealing himself in mercy to Saul of Tarsus. Saul then became a prolific writer and apostle. Stephen's loss was leveraged into great gains for the Kingdom of God.

When Paul was lost to public ministry by being jailed for years, God "leveraged" the loss of his public ministry by having him write the epistles from prison that are such a major part of the New Testament. Paul also wrote, "And because of my chains, most of the brothers and sisters have become confident in the Lord and dare all the more to proclaim the gospel without fear," (Phil. 1:14).

It is important to remember that God can leverage a "loss" to his kingdom in several ways. He can leverage the loss into a great gain of heavenly treasure and eternal glory (see 2 Cor. 4:17). He can leverage the loss into a great gain of souls through evangelism. He could leverage the loss into great financial gain on this earth as he did for Job (Job 42:12-16). But he can also leverage a loss into massive judgment against wicked people who refuse to repent.

When the apostle James was martyred, his loss was leveraged into great judgment. King Herod was directly responsible for ordering James to be killed with the sword. God did not strike King Herod with a bolt of mercy. Instead, a holy angel struck him so that worms were suddenly seen eating his body and *then* he died. He didn't die and have his body eaten by worms, as in normal decay. No, the worms of hell came up to greet this wicked man. His death was the most shameful ever. He was struck down in front of a crowd of people who had been proclaiming him to be a god. He was eaten by worms in front of them before his soul descended into hell. (See Acts 12:23)

We should desire and pray that our pain, invested in the bank of heaven, will have the end result of giving God the right to strike people with bolts of mercy and turn them into righteous people as he did to Saul of Tarsus. However, God knows the hearts of all people. Those who would never repent will be struck with bolts of judgment, terrible leveraged judgment as in the case of King Herod.

Paul wrote, Do not take revenge, my dear friends, but leave room for God's wrath, for it is written: "It is mine to avenge; I will repay," says the Lord. (Romans 12:19) Since God knows who will repent and who will never repent, we leave room for the possibility that our loss might be leveraged into great judgment that would cause others to fear God and find salvation in Christ.

15

SEE THEM AS A VICTIM OF SATAN AND DON'T VIEW YOURSELF AS THE VICTIM

See *them* as *victims* or captives of Satan.

THE PERSON WHO wronged you was a captive of Satan. Satan took them captive to do his will. If you view them as captives of Satan, then you'll know that they are the victims, not you. That makes it a lot easier to feel sorry for them and forgive them. Satan treats his captives horribly! His one desire is to drag them all the way to an eternity in hell to suffer forever with him in torment.

Paul wrote, "And the Lord's servant must not be quarrelsome but must be kind to everyone, able to teach, not resentful. Opponents must be gently instructed, in the hope that God will grant them repentance leading them to a knowledge of the truth, and that they will come to their senses and escape from the trap of the devil, who has taken them captive to do his will" (2 Tim. 2:24–26).

Paul used this technique and passed it on to Timothy. Those who oppose the godly are actually captives of Satan. They have been taken captive and forced to do the devil's will.

Jesus used this same technique. He saw in advance that Peter would deny him three times and even deny him with an oath. But Jesus didn't say, "Simon, you jerk! You are going to deny that you know me. You are even going to curse and deny me with an oath! What kind of a friend are you? I'm so offended!" No, Jesus did not say that.

Instead, Jesus said, "Simon, Simon, Satan has asked to sift you as wheat. But I have prayed for you, Simon, that your faith may not fail. And when you have turned back, strengthen your brothers" (Luke 22:31–32).

Jesus didn't see himself as a victim of Peter's denial. He saw Peter as a victim of Satan. Who is the victim, the person who wronged you or you? You decide. Then, say out loud, "I'm not the victim here. They are." When we view the person who did wrong to us as a captive of Satan, trapped and forced to do his will, it's a lot easier for us to forgive. It also helps us to avoid developing a victim mentality.

VENT FRUSTRATIONS THROUGH POSITIVE PRAYER

Praying for those who mistreat you releases negative emotions.

I N BIBLE COLLEGE, some dorm mates were making homemade root beer in a pressure cooker. The pressure relief valve would not work to release pressure in the pot. Those who were with me upstairs in this dormitory heard running footsteps downstairs. We heard the door slam. Then we heard a huge explosion. We ran down to see the kitchen dripping in root beer, the curtains blown down, and a hole the size of the pressure cooker lid in the kitchen ceiling!

When the pressure relief valve stuck and would not work, the needle of the pressure gauge went to the end of the red zone. The root beer makers tried to knock the lid off. The handles broke off, thus sparing them from getting scalded. When they saw it was going to explode they ran for their lives. What a memory!

Like the pressure cooker, we need a pressure relief valve that works. Jesus told us how to have an effective pressure relief valve for our souls. "But to you who are listening I say: Love your enemies, do good to those who hate you, bless those who curse you, pray for those who mistreat you" (Luke 6:27–28).

Praying positive prayers for those who have done you wrong releases YOUR (it says our) destructive emotional pressures so that you won't explode in anger or suffer a serious health crisis. God taught me that if a person irritated me more than any other person, that was the person I should pray for the most. As long as we follow God's advice, our pressure relief valves are working. If we don't pray for the people who irritate us, emotional pressures will build up dangerously inside of us.

Jesus said, "Pray for those who persecute you" (Matt. 5:44). He's not just concerned for that persecutor. He's concerned for us, as well. Our prayers for them will benefit them and also free us from the pressure of negative emotions.

DO SOMETHING GOOD FOR THEM

Paul wrote:

Do not repay anyone evil for evil. Be careful to do what is right in the eyes of everyone. If it is possible, as far as it depends on you, live at peace with everyone. Do not take revenge, my dear friends, but leave room for God's wrath, for it is written: "It is mine to avenge; I will repay," says the Lord. On the contrary: "If your enemy is hungry, feed him; if he is thirsty, give him something to drink. In doing this, you will heap burning coals on his head." Do not be overcome by evil, but overcome evil with good."

(Rom. 12:17–21)

MAY 31, 1981, I started a church in Omaha, Nebraska. Fifteen years later that church went through a massive church split that lasted about seven months. Finally, I was able to turn the church over to another pastor, and I became an evangelist. Every day God would bring a certain man to my mind. He had been a deacon and had taken sides with a staff member I had fired. He was a principle player in the church split.

Every time God brought him to my mind I would do three things: I would pray for him, forgive him, and bless him. This went on for weeks, and finally I wondered why God kept bringing him back to my mind. I reminded the Lord that I was no longer the pastor, that the church split was now months behind me, water under the bridge, so to speak. I reminded God that I was faithfully praying for this man, expressing forgiveness, and even blessing him. Still God kept bringing him back to my mind. So one day I asked, "Lord, what more do you want me to do?"

The FEAST of FORGIVENESS

#1 Forgive Them
= Just plain forgiveness is like plain spaghetti.

#2 Bless Them
= Forgiveness is getting tastier.

#3 Pray for Them
= Forgiveness is getting really nourishing.

#4 Do Good to Them
= Now forgiveness is a tasty feast!

God impressed these words into my spirit, "Do good to him." So I helped him get a $6,000 grant for a summer ministry he had in Latin America. He responded by hosting a farewell party for me and invited everyone who had left the church. Most of the people who had left came to that party and embraced my family and me. It was a wonderful miracle of reconciliation and came about when I did something good for a man who had been a leader in the split.

Not many people like to eat plain spaghetti. It would be a pretty bland meal. But it would improve if you added tomato sauce. It would improve even more if you added meatballs. It would become a tasty feast if you added Parmesan cheese.

In the same way, the feast of forgiveness requires four actions. Jesus said, "Love your enemies, do good to those who hate you, bless those who curse you, pray for those who mistreat you" (Luke 6:27–28). If you want a real feast of forgiveness, first forgive that person. Then ask God to bless them. Pray a loving prayer for them, doing your best to pray something good into his or her life. Finally, actually do something good for that person. By doing these four things, your mind and spirit will have a feast of forgiveness complete with joy, peace, kindness and love.

In my opinion, few Christians ever get to the "feast of forgiveness" because they leave out one or more of these four things. If you'll do all four, you will experience the full feast of forgiveness Jesus intends for you.

18

FORGIVE FOR THE LORD'S SAKE

CRIPTURES TELL US that we can do certain things for the Lord's sake. Here are two examples.

Peter wrote, "Submit yourselves for the Lord's sake to every human authority" (1 Peter 2:13).

Paul wrote, "That is why, for Christ's sake, I delight in weaknesses, in insults, in hardships, in persecutions, in difficulties. For when I am weak, then I am strong" (2 Cor. 12:10).

I once wrote a letter to someone sharing a desire of my heart. That person wrote me back and thoroughly condemned me for having that desire. It was a perfectly righteous desire, yet I was condemned for having it. Even worse, this person prejudged me and told me if I held on to this desire, I'd surely become something very evil.

I've had lots of insults, but I considered this the greatest insult I have ever received. I have never been able to even imagine anything more offensive. I was so angry I felt I could bite a nail in half.

Jesus spoke to me, "Can you forgive her for her sake?"

I said, "*No!*"

Then he said, "Can you forgive her for *my* sake?"

I pictured Jesus dying on the cross to save her. He was doing everything in his power to get her forgiven. Yet I had been ready to hold an offense against her forever.

When I realized I would be working directly against all the Lord was trying to do if I held onto unforgiveness, I said, "Well, for your sake, yes. I can forgive her." And I did. The greatest offense I've ever received was detoxified just like that! It never bothered me again. Best of all, I've had a very warm and lasting relationship with that person.

19

CLAIM THEM AS YOUR VERY OWN

"Father, I claim them for my spiritual inheritance!"

AS A YOUNG associate pastor, I got to preach one Sunday at our church. One third of the way through the message, the anointing of God came upon me with power, and I really *preached*. That next week my wife heard that brother so-and-so thought I was showing off. She said, "Brother so-and-so doesn't like you."

I immediately said, "If he doesn't like me, then I don't like him."

Instantly the Holy Spirit said to me, "You'd love him if he rode your bus." I agreed. I knew that was true. But why?

I was a bus captain, meaning that I used a bus to bring little children to church. I visited about 120 children per week on that route and almost always had 60 or more on my bus. I worked so hard to get those children to come to church. I loved each one of them, even though many were little rascals. I knew if this older man rode my bus, I'd love him just like I loved those badly behaved children. I also knew that if he just drove his car to church I would not love him. He would not be "mine."

Then I remembered Donny and Ronny, two red-haired, four-year-old, hyperactive twins. They rode my wife's bus. When they got off the bus, one would run across the street, giggling, and dive into the bushes. One would run underneath a row of nine large buses where he could have banged his head on a muffler.

One day a deacon was chasing one of those little boys down the hallway. The little guy turned into the church office and the deacon chased him around and around a table. Then the boy dived under the table and bit the deacon on the leg. He also called him a bad six-letter curse word.

That week, the deacon, the children's pastor, and the lead pastor all came to me and said, "Tell your wife not to bring Donny and Ronny any more. They are too disruptive. We can't lose the entire Sunday school for the sake of those two boys."

When I relayed the message to my wife that she was not allowed to bring Donny and Ronny any more, she burst into tears. "They can't do that," she sobbed. "They are *my* kids. You don't know how hard their home life is!"

I told her she had to do something different and from that day on, she'd hold their hands as they got off the bus. She'd take one to the three-year old room and take the other to the four-year old room. She'd sit with that one until the teachers got his attention and then go back into the three-year old room to help control the other one. Bonnie missed the adult morning worship service for six months as she worked to help little Donny and Ronny. Then their mother came to church and received Christ as her Savior. Loving persistence paid off!

As I thought about this, God brought the words of Jesus to my mind, "Father, all Thine are mine" (John 17:10 KJV). I realized that if I claimed brother so-and-so as my very own, I'd love him, even if he was being somewhat of a rascal like Donny and Ronny. We fight for those whom we claim as our own, not against them. When I claimed him as my own, I liked him, and soon he liked me. I never had to forgive him for not liking me because I claimed him as my very own.

20

DID YOU LAY A STUMBLING BLOCK FOR THEM?

URING THE YEARS I have served as a lead pastor, I've often given couples Dr. Willard Harley's great book, *His Needs, Her Needs*. Each chapter begins with the story of a couple trying to save their marriage after either the husband or the wife had committed adultery. I liked to give this book to young couples *before* they got married in hopes of preventing marital breakups.

In each case history, Dr. Harley helped the offended mate to see that they had not been meeting the emotional needs of their mate. By not meeting their mate's emotional needs, they were laying a stumbling stone in front of their husband or wife. Most of these marriages were saved when the offended mate repented for laying a stumbling stone, and the adulterous mate repented and broke off the affair. Then they each concentrated on understanding and meeting each other's emotional needs.

There is no excuse for stumbling over a stumbling stone. Jesus said, "Anyone who walks in the daytime will not stumble, for they see by this world's light. It is when a person walks at night that they stumble, for they have no light" (John 11:9–10). Why would a person commit adultery? Because they are not walking in the light! If they walked in the light of God's Word, they would walk around the stumbling stone. They could even make it a stepping stone! People fall into sin because they are walking in darkness.

However, the Lord will hold people who lay stumbling blocks in someone's path responsible for their own sins. Laying a stumbling block in someone's path is very serious.

Jesus also said, "And whosoever shall cause one of these little ones that believe on me to stumble, it were better for him if a great millstone were hanged about his neck, and he were cast into the sea" (Mark 9:42 ASV).

Here's my point. It is easier to forgive someone for stumbling if you, yourself, are the one who put the stumbling stone in his or her path. A wife or husband's failure to meet the emotional needs of a mate doesn't justify the adulterous mate. Remember, if they walked in the light, they would not have stumbled. But the sobering reality that you may have laid the stumbling stone they stumbled over makes it a lot easier to forgive.

A scriptural example is the story of Judah and Tamar from Genesis 38. Judah got a wife for his oldest son. But that young man was so wicked the Lord put him to death. So Tamar was given to the next oldest son. He, too, was wicked and the Lord put him to death. Judah was afraid of giving Tamar to his youngest son for fear harm would come to him also. So he told Tamar to wait until the young boy got older.

After several years Tamar realized that Judah would never give her to his youngest son who had now grown up. In those days, there was no government program to take care of the elderly. You had to have children to rely on in your old age. So Tamar did something desperate. She disguised herself as a prostitute and sat along the road where her father-in-law would pass by on his way to shear sheep.

Judah saw a veiled lady by the road and assumed she was a prostitute. He had no payment with him, but agreed to give her his staff and seal until he came back with a young goat so she had sex with him. Tamar did not wait for the young goat as payment. Instead, she took off her disguise and went home. Judah's friend came back with the goat, but found no roadside prostitute.

Three months later it was told Judah, "Your daughter is pregnant and is guilty of prostitution."

Judah said, "Bring her out and have her burned alive."

Before they could kill her she held up Judah's staff and seal and said, "I am pregnant by the man who owns these.

See if you recognize whose seal and staff and cord these are" (Gen. 38:25).

Judah recognized them and said, "She is more righteous than I, since I wouldn't give her to my son Shelah" (Gen. 38:26).

One minute Judah was ready to have Tamar burned at the stake. Then he saw that he was the one who had laid a stumbling stone in her path. It changed his viewpoint immediately. Tamar was allowed to live and she gave birth to twins who became famous in the tribe of Judah.

Paul wrote, "Do not cause anyone to stumble, whether Jews, Greeks or the church of God" (1 Cor. 10:32). Remember, if someone puts a stumbling stone in your path, it will not justify your sinning. You will not stumble if you are walking in the light. If you do stumble and sin, you'll be held responsible for not walking in the light.

Ask yourself if you might have somehow laid a stumbling block in someone's path. If your mate has sinned against you, it doesn't prove that you laid a stumbling block in front of him or her. Some people stumble over the stumbling blocks they have placed in their own paths. Don't let the devil advise you. Ask the Holy Spirit if you are guilty of laying down a stumbling stone. If so, humble yourself and repent for your own sin. Then it will be much easier to forgive the person who stumbled in sin against you.

21

IF GOD HAS FAILED YOUR EXPECTATIONS, HE IS DOING SOMETHING GREATER THAN YOU UNDERSTAND

MANY PEOPLE ARE angry at God for allowing various painful things to come into their lives. Others are greatly disappointed with God because he did not grant some prayer that they fervently asked and believed for. God never fails, but he sometimes fails to do what we are expecting. This can crush the human spirit. This is much more than a broken heart. The positive expectations of the heart are crushed into a thousand pieces.

This happened to me. God failed my expectations because he was skipping over them to do something bigger and better, but I did not understand this. My disappointment was extremely painful, emotionally. I no longer wanted to pray about anything. The Holy Spirit came to my rescue and showed me truths from God's Word that healed my crushed spirit.

Understand this: You may be bitter at God, but you cannot forgive God. If someone says, "You need to forgive God," that is an erroneous concept, a misnomer. God never sins. He never fails. He never does anything wrong. He is not morally inferior to us, and he will never need our forgiveness. We need his understanding.

Mary and Martha were deeply disappointed with Jesus. They had notified him that their brother was seriously ill. They really believed Jesus would come at once and heal their brother. Yet Jesus did not come until their brother had been in the tomb for four days. Jesus intended to do something bigger. He raised Lazarus from the dead, thus making the Pharisees so jealous that they put into motion the plan to crucify him. By allowing himself to be crucified, Jesus paid the price of redemption for the entire world. He thinks bigger than we do. They were thinking, "Heal my brother." He was thinking, "Redeem the world."

Jacob had twelve sons, and the second to the youngest was his favorite. He sent Joseph on an errand to see how the older boys were doing. Jacob no doubt prayed and asked God to protect Joseph and bring him home safe. Instead, a bloody robe was presented to Jacob. "We found this," the brothers said. "Examine it to see if it is your son's robe" (Gen. 37:32).

Jacob was overwhelmed with grief. For something like the next seventeen years he was no longer a man of faith. He became a whiney old man, one who had a crushed spirit. No one could comfort him. Jacob thought God had failed him (Gen. 37:35).

However, many years later Joseph's brothers went down to Egypt to buy grain because of the severe famine in the land. Jacob did not send the youngest son with them because he was afraid that harm would come to him as it did to Joseph. Joseph, who had become the governor of Egypt and the most powerful man next to the Pharaoh, recognized his brothers, but he did not reveal his identity to them. He knew that his younger brother Benjamin was not with them, and so he accused them of being spies and demanded that they go back home and bring the younger brother to him to prove him wrong. Joseph kept his brother Simeon in prison while they traveled home. They eventually came back with Benjamin when their food ran out. Eventually Joseph revealed himself to them and told them he held no ill-will towards them. He forgave them and told them this was God's plan to save them and the whole family. The brothers traveled back home and told their father Jacob, "Joseph is alive. In fact, he is the ruler of Egypt!" Jacob was stunned; he did not believe them. But when they told him everything Joseph had said to them and when he saw the carts Joseph had sent to carry him back, the spirit of their father Jacob revived. And Israel [Jacob] said "I'm convinced! My son Joseph is still alive. I will go and see him before I die" (Gen. 45:26–28).

Notice, when Jacob's heart revived, he once again became that spiritual man God had named *Israel*, the man of faith, the man who had wrestled with God and won!

Jacob had probably prayed, "Bring my boy home safe." God had skipped over that prayer because it was too small. Instead, God did something exceedingly greater. He took Joseph to Egypt and trained him in administration. First he administered the affairs of a wealthy man, and then he administered a prison. After that, God had him administer the affairs of Egypt, and finally he administered the sale of food to people from an entire region.

Because Joseph had such favor with Pharaoh, he was able to give the best of Egypt, the land of Goshen, to Jacob's descendants. There in Egypt, God multiplied them until they became a nation. Then through Moses, God took them to be his special witness nation to the world, the nation through which he would bring the Redeemer, Jesus Christ, the Savior of the world. See how differently God thinks? He thinks far bigger than you and I do.

God plays checkers with the devil.

I hope you are familiar with the simple game of checkers. The master checker player controls the game by the checkers he sacrifices or loses in order to get in a better position to take the opponent's checker pieces. By forcing the opponent to jump one of his checkers he positions the board, double jumps the enemy, and opens up the king row. Then he says, "King me."

Imagine a little checker being moved into harm's way. He gets jumped by the enemy and removed from the board! He wonders, "Why did my very own master allow the enemy to jump me and remove me from the game? Doesn't he love me anymore?"

The master is being faithful all the time. He is in full control of the game even when it doesn't look like it. Soon, he double-jumps the opponent, opens up the king row, and says, "King me!" Suddenly the little checker piece which was lost earlier in the game is picked up and placed on top of another checker, becoming a king. Then he says, "Ahhh. Now I understand. My master was being faithful all the time. He was outsmarting the enemy. Now I have a brand new anointing! I'm a king! I can move backwards, forwards, and sideways!"

David was anointed to become king of Israel. But before he became king, he faced many trials. King Saul was afraid of David because the Lord was with David, and he became his enemy. Saul was relentless in pursuing David to kill him. So David decided to escape from him by going to the land of the Philistines with his army of six hundred men (1 Sam. 27:1). The son of the king of Gath gave Ziklag to David and his army as a place to live. When the Philistines gathered together to fight against Israel, David wanted to go to battle with the Philistines against Israel and the army of King Saul. The Philistine commanders were afraid David would turn on them in battle so they convinced the king to not let him join in the battle. David was sent back to his home town, Ziklag.

When David and his six hundred men returned, they
found their town was burned, their property stolen, and their

families all taken captive. They wept until they had no more strength to weep. God had allowed David and his men to be "jumped" by the enemy. However, God used this to promote David to the kingship. After hearing an encouraging word from God, David led his men in pursuit, attacked the enemy, and recovered everything. They also recovered so much plunder that David sent gifts to the elders of Judah.

Meanwhile, God had forsaken the evil King Saul, and he had been killed in battle. His headless body was nailed to the wall of a heathen temple. During this time of crisis, the elders of Judah received gifts of treasure from David saying, "Here is a gift for you from the plunder of the Lord's enemies" (1 Sam. 30:26). God was obviously helping David, and Saul was dead. The elders thought, "Why not make David our new king?" Soon David was king in Hebron.

I could write an entire book of examples of people who were first disappointed with God only to later understand that when he skipped over the small thing they were believing for, he was doing something much bigger and more glorious. What does it look like to you now? Are you still like the little checker by the side of the board wondering why God allowed you to be jumped by the enemy? If you could just understand what God is doing, you'd see that somehow, he will exalt you. Jesus said, "Blessed are those who are persecuted because of righteousness, for theirs is the kingdom of heaven" (Matt. 5:10). Keep the faith! You will sit enthroned with Jesus! (Rev. 3:21). Bigger things than you could imagine are being done on your behalf. Your Master is forever faithful. He is the Alpha and the Omega, the first and the last. He moves first, he moves last, and he always wins! When you understand the bigger thing God is doing or has done, your heart will revive like Jacob's heart. Once again you will be a strong man or woman of faith.

The greatest example of this principle is that of Jesus Christ. God the Father allowed the Jews and Romans to crucify Jesus. He was jumped and removed from the checker board, so to speak. His body lay in the tomb until the third day. "Therefore God exalted him to the highest place and gave him a name above every other name, that at the name of Jesus, every knee shall bow in heaven and in earth and under the earth, and every tongue acknowledge that Jesus Christ is Lord, to the glory of the Father" (Phil. 2:9–11).

CONCLUSION: DESIRE TO BE LIKE CHRIST

P AUL WROTE, "I want to know Christ—yes, to know the power of his resurrection and participation in his sufferings, becoming like him in his death, and so, somehow, attaining to the resurrection from the dead" (Phil. 3:10–11). What does it mean to want to be like Christ in his death? Paul meant that he wanted to die forgiving people, just as Jesus did. Christ died without anger, bitterness, or self-pity. Christ also died trusting his spirit into the hands of the Father, even though it looked like God had forsaken him. Would you like to be like Christ in his death? In both life and death, Jesus lived without bitterness, unforgiveness, or self-pity. He died believing his Father would make everything right!

Jesus forgives everyone who comes to him in repentance and faith. He wants you to be like him. If you imitate Jesus in life and death, your fellowship with him will always be close and intimate.

The devil never forgives anything. Would you like to become like the devil or become like Jesus in his death, living and dying free from bitterness and unforgiveness? Express your desire to God saying, "Father, I do want to live like Jesus and when I die, I'd like to be like Jesus in his death and be free from bitterness and unforgiveness."

Desire to Be Like Jesus Christ

It didn't take very long for you to read this little book. But it will take the grace of God for you to live these truths until they become habitual. I hope you will go through these pages several times and make each technique of forgiveness your very own. Ask the Holy Spirit to be your spiritual coach who will help you with the day-to-day application of these truths.

Finally, if I am still alive on earth when you read this book, please pray for me. Teachers are judged more strictly (James 3:1). If I have helped you, please help me by praying that the Holy Spirit will guide me to live these truths so that God may be glorified through my life. If someone else teaches you this material, pray for your teacher! We need each other. I'm keenly aware of my need for your love and prayers. Please pray for my descendants, asking that they, too, would have God's grace to guide them in obedience to all the teachings of Jesus Christ.

"Father, I know that everyone who reads this book has been wronged in life. Each one has suffered some injustice. Some have suffered far more than others. Those who haven't suffered much yet will have to pass through future times of pain. My prayer is that you will help each one of them practice these truths. May every toxic emotion be dissolved into peace. Please help the practice of these truths to become so habitual that future events will not cause them to stumble. May they always walk in the light of your Word. Give them so much spiritual dignity that they can overlook offenses, drop matters of contention, and bear with one another in love. Please treasure their pain as an investment in the Bank of Heaven and give them amazing spiritual dividends. Help each one to climb out of the Cistern of Sadness and find joy in helping others. May they all overcome through your grace and enjoy the feast of forgiveness.

"And now, Father, may people all around the world be helped through the lives of those who read and practice these truths. We think of all the suffering and hurting people in the world. As you help us keep a Christ-like attitude through all the trials of life, please flow through us and use each of us to help multitudes of other people for your eternal glory. Holy Spirit of God, empower me to be a forgiving person."

Do you agree with that prayer? Tell the Lord: "Father, I do agree with that prayer. And together we ask that in Jesus' name."

I love you.
May God bless you.

TO ORDER ADDITIONAL COPIES OF THIS BOOK PLEASE CONTACT AUTHOR WES DAUGHENBAUGH:

We'd love to have you teach this material in a small group or class setting. We discount these books to just $5 each and when you order fifteen books we'll GIVE you a free 78 minute DVD of Wes teaching through the book in 31 short "chapters." A teacher should play two or three of these (about nine minutes) and then use the rest of the class for discussion, prayer and extra study from all the material in the FREE Teacher's Guide (E-book).

A student workbook (E-book) can be downloaded for just $1 from www.EncouragementExpert.com. Those who order fifteen books will be given a FREE student workbook (E-book). Prices are subject to change.

This offer is only available through Gospel Net Ministries.

Our phone: 541-729-5015 E-mail: EncouragementExpert@gmail.com
Gospel Net Ministries, PO Box 485, Creswell, OR 97426

For information about the other books by Wes Daughenbaugh, complete with DVD sets, Teacher's Guides and Student workbooks go to www.EncouragementExpert.com.

THE HEART GOD HEARS
You can be the heart that God always hears!
(Wes has based his life and ministry on the truths in this unique book.)

GOOD AND FAITHFUL SERVANT
A Trumpet Call To Return To Spiritual Leadership

This book will train you to be a spiritual leader empowered by THE LEADER of the church, the Holy Spirit. It is illustrated with 63 professional drawings. You can bring massive glory to God! You can lead many to righteousness!

Sign up for the free online monthly newsletter that connects to Wes's POD CAST at www.EncouragementExpert.com.